Copycat

Nature-Inspired Design Around the World

Christy Hale

Lee & Low Books Inc.   New York

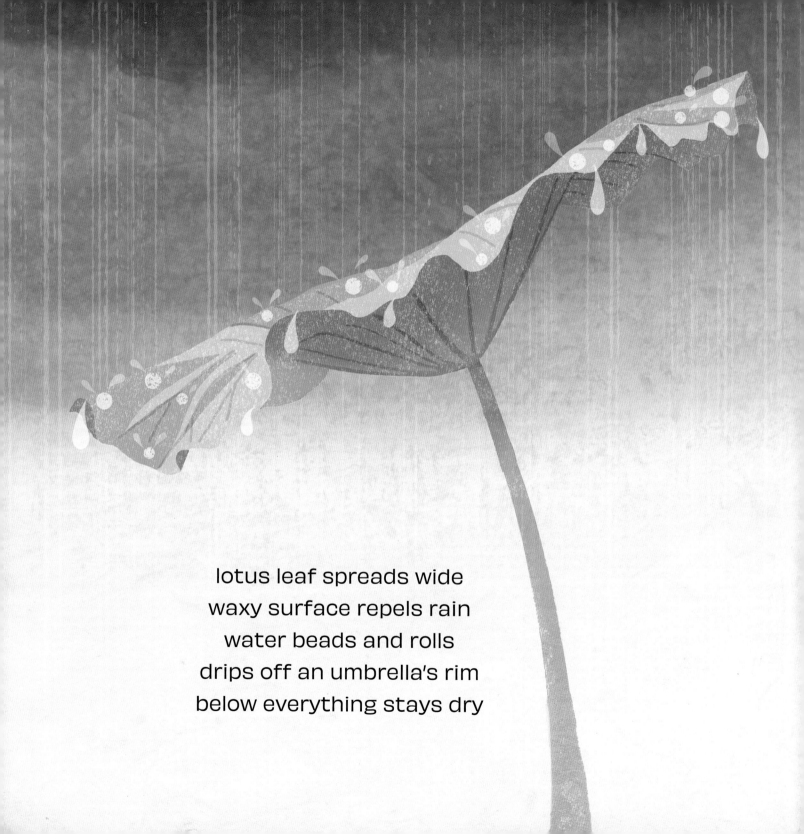

lotus leaf spreads wide
waxy surface repels rain
water beads and rolls
drips off an umbrella's rim
below everything stays dry

UMBRELLA: Waterproof covering provides protection from rain.

agile dragonfly
shifts and darts every which way
with two sets of wings
whirlybird lifts, glides, hovers
master of flight maneuvers

HELICOPTER: Rotating blades allow flight in many directions.

baobab branches
catch sunlight and scarce raindrops
funnel resources
and offer them out again
colossal tree-like structures

VERTICAL GARDEN: Tall structures collect rainwater and produce solar energy.

on desert mornings
thirsty beetle leans and waits
then foggy mist clings
dew-covered bottle drips, saves
water for a welcome drink

WATER BOTTLE: Cold metal surface condenses water from dewdrops.

diving kingfisher
needle beak breaks through water
with barely a sound
speedy, streamlined railroad train
it's hard to hear it coming

BULLET TRAIN: Tapered train nose reduces noise at high speeds

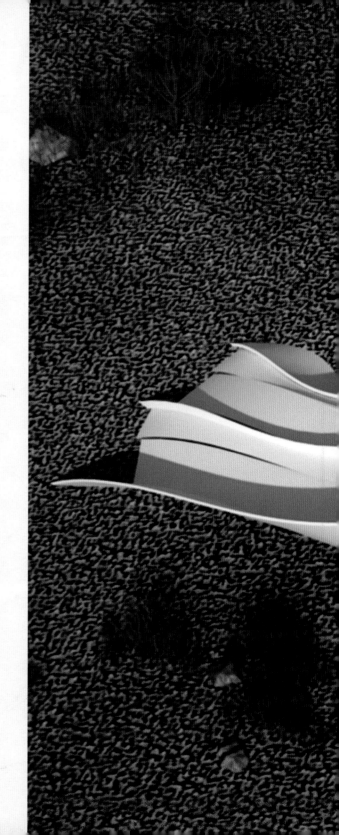

earth too hot to touch
snail beats the heat and withdraws
high into its shell
deep inside a desert home
a self-cooling space to live

DESERT DWELLING: High, curved panels create naturally air-cooled space.

tiny hummingbird
up, down it flutters, twists, lifts
power in its wings
tall, strong wind converter makes
quiet electricity

WIND CONVERTER: Flapping wings turn wind power into energy.

termite architects
build mounds with ventilation
giant breathing lungs
in tunnels, vents, and chimneys
air heats or cools a high rise

BUILDING COMPLEX: Nature-based ventilation system uses less energy.

prickly burrs grab tight
to anything passing by
little hooks and loops
join with a powerful grip
separate sides bind as one

HOOK AND LOOP FASTENER: Hooks and loops interlock for strong, reversible bond.

shy armadillo
overlapping scales rolled tight
a snug little ball
folds up so efficiently
car needs hardly any space

FOLD-UP CAR: Rear of car tucks over front to park in small spaces.

sponges and corals
dine on tiny particles
filter surroundings
building's shell screens out the smog
making fresh and healthy air

SMOG-EATING SHELL: Surface tiles filter out air pollutants and break down smog.

long octopus arm
tapered tool with suction cups
stretches, coils, and holds
robot tentacle gripper
makes factory work safer

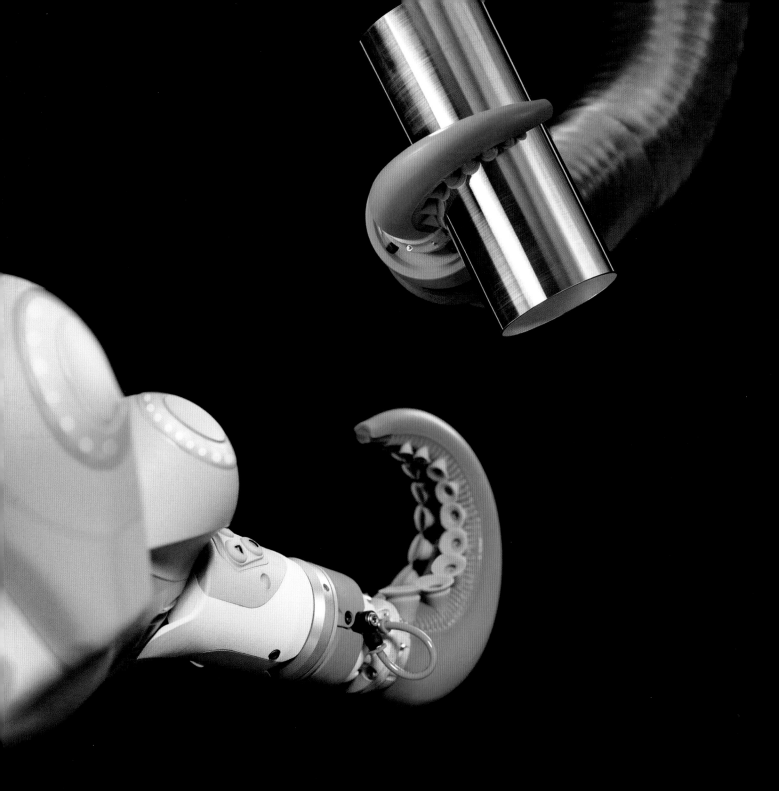

ROBOTIC ARM: Flexible tentacle grasps, lifts, and moves objects of different shapes.

icicle cavern
stalactites and stalagmites
hang down and rise up
outdoor urban public space
relief from the summer heat

URBAN SPACE: Gently dripping water creates cool, cave-like environment.

honeycomb bee cells
fit together—neat, compact
space-saving structure
modular blocks join to make
homes for many families

HOUSING PROJECT: Space-efficient design makes for eco-friendly homes.

in the dark of night
cat eyes glow like little stars
bright spots of light shine
in the headlight beams of cars
guide drivers along dim roads

ROAD REFLECTOR: Safety device lights up traffic lane boundaries.

See **CAT EYES/ROAD REFLECTOR** to learn how cat eyes inspired the invention of reflecting devices that improve road safety.

"Look deep

into nature,

and then

you will

understand

everything

better."

—Albert Einstein

LOTUS LEAF

Lotus plants rise above the surface of muddy ponds and lakes on tall stalks. Their almost perfectly round, disc-like leaves can spread out to nearly 3 feet (91 centimeters) in diameter. Lotus leaves are water repellent. Their surface is covered with small bumps or ridges and a layer of wax, causing water to bead up and roll off. As water moves across the leaves, it also washes away particles of dirt, allowing photosynthesis to occur.

UMBRELLA

There are many legends about the creation and use of umbrellas. One legend says that children taking cover from the rain below large lotus leaves may have inspired the invention of the waterproof umbrella almost four thousand years ago in China. Over the centuries, the umbrella, or parasol, developed as a collapsible canopy on a handheld pole used mostly as a shield from the sun. The modern umbrella for protection from rain is believed to have been invented by Englishman Jonas Hanway in 1750.

DRAGONFLY

Dragonflies have two sets of wings, providing them with four nearly identical wings that they can move independently of one another. When moving forward, their two front wings provide lift and their two rear wings provide momentum. Dragonflies can switch quickly to move in reverse, using their rear wings for lift and their front wings for momentum. Dragonflies can also move straight up and down, turn sharply, and stop and hover in place.

HELICOPTER

On September 14, 1939, Igor Sikorsky, a Russian-born engineer, flew the world's first practical helicopter in Stratford, Connecticut. To make his VS-300 helicopter light enough, Sikorsky used a single main rotor and one small tail rotor. Although the flight lasted only ten seconds, it showed that the helicopter could be controlled. With modern advances, today's helicopters can take off and land vertically, fly forward and backward, and hover for long periods of time—just like a dragonfly.

BAOBAB

Baobab trees are found in dry areas of Madagascar, mainland Africa, the Arabian Peninsula, and Australia. Baobabs grow to enormous sizes and can survive for thousands of years. Known as the "Tree of Life," a baobab provides water, food, and shelter for humans and animals. The huge trunk can store up to 32,000 gallons (120,000 liters) of water and the hollow trunk of an old tree can provide shelter.

VERTICAL GARDEN

In 2012, a human-made forest of eighteen giant tree-like structures, called supertrees, opened along Singapore's Marina Bay. The supertrees resemble baobabs and are designed like natural trees. The trunks are a vertical garden of vines, ferns, and flowers that absorb and collect rainwater. In addition, the supertrees have branches that spread out at the top, creating wide surfaces for shelter and solar panels that produce solar power. This creates self-sustaining, renewable energy.

DESERT BEETLE

The Namib Desert is one of the driest places on Earth, so Namib Desert beetles must be efficient water collectors. On foggy mornings the beetles go to the peaks of the sand dunes and raise their backs up into the fog. The small ridges and bumps on their backs help the beetles collect condensed water droplets out of the fog. Namib Desert beetles can store up to forty percent of their body weight in water daily.

KINGFISHER

A kingfisher often hunts from a perch above a river, lake, or stream. When a fish is spotted, the bird dives suddenly at high speed, straight down into the water to capture its prey. Although the bird has a large head, its long, tapering beak allows for a smooth transition from the air into the water. The kingfisher enters the water with minimal splash, so there is little disturbance to drive away the fish and a greater chance of a successful catch.

SNAIL

Some snail species are able to stay cool even in the high temperatures of dry, hot deserts. The curved outer surface of the snail's shell reflects sunlight and heat. The largest whorl, or spiral, of the shell touches the cooler soil under the snail only in some places. This leaves a layer of air between the shell and the soil. The air in this space slows down heat flow into the snail. When the snail gets too hot, it retreats deep into the uppermost whorls of its shell, where the temperature is lower.

HUMMINGBIRD

Most birds fly with upstrokes and downstrokes of their wings, with the downstrokes providing lift. But hummingbirds sweep their wings forward and backward and can rotate and twist their wings at the shoulder. This creates a horizontal figure eight pattern with each wing beat and generates lift. The figure eight motion also keeps hummingbirds in the air and lets them hover in place. Hummingbirds can fly forward, backward, up, down, and upside down.

WATER BOTTLE

In 2010, Kitae Pak, a Korean inventor, developed a water-harvesting bottle to address water scarcity in dry climates. Mimicking the form of the Namib Desert beetle, Pak's Dew Bank Bottle has a sloping, ribbed dome. When placed outside at night, the stainless steel dome becomes colder than the air. As the air warms in the morning, dew forms on the cool metal. The dew droplets are channeled over the dome and collected in the bottle, producing clean drinking water.

BULLET TRAIN

The first high-speed (bullet) trains were introduced in Japan in the 1960s. The high speeds caused atmospheric pressure waves to build up in front of the trains, causing loud booms when they exited tunnels. In 1997, Eiji Nakatsu, an engineer for the West Japan Railway Company, found a way to decrease the noise. Nakatsu observed that a kingfisher dives into water with very little splash and noise. After he redesigned the bullet train nose to imitate the bird's streamlined beak, trains ran faster, more quietly, and used less energy.

DESERT DWELLING

In 2012, Elnaz Amiri, Hesam Andalib, Roza Atarod, and M-amin Mohamadi, students from the Art University of Isfahan in Iran, won the Biomimicry Institute's Student Design Competition with their plan for a self-cooling desert dwelling. The off-white exterior reflects sunlight. Curved, overlapping panels imitate the whorls of a snail's shell to create a dwelling that becomes cooler and cooler the farther inside you go. The home is comfortable even in extremely hot climates.

WIND CONVERTER

In Tunisia, the Tyer Wind company developed a wind converter inspired by the hummingbird. Introduced in 2016, the converter has "wings" that harness energy from the wind by imitating the figure eight motion of a hovering hummingbird. The captured energy is renewable, allowing for electricity that does not rely on fossil fuels. The wings have a smaller sweep area compared to other wind converters, making the Tyer Wind converter more compact, quieter, less conspicuous, and safer for migrating birds.

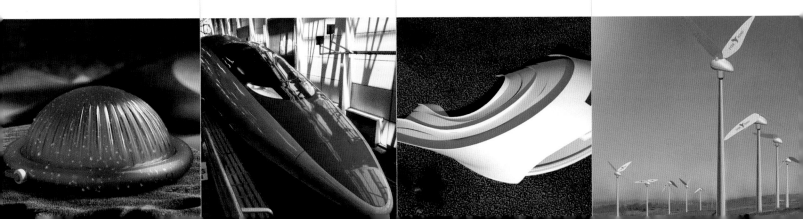

TERMITE MOUND

Some termite species in Zimbabwe construct a tall mound above their underground nest. The nest is where the termites farm a fungus that must be kept at precisely 87°F (30°C). Outside temperature can shift from near freezing at night to more than 100°F (38°C) during the day. The termites regulate the temperature by opening and plugging up a network of heating and cooling vents. This creates currents that pull air in at the bottom of the mound and release it at the top.

BUILDING COMPLEX

Eastgate Centre, Zimbabwe's largest office and shopping complex, opened in 1996. The designer, Mick Pearce, created this tropical structure without standard air-conditioning and heating. Instead, he mimicked the ventilation system of a termite mound. Air from outside is cooled or warmed by the building mass, vented onto the floors, and then released through chimneys at the top. This creates an energy-efficient structure, saving both the environment and reducing costs for the tenants.

BURRS

Plants cannot move, so some have evolved special ways to scatter their seeds. *Arctium*, a plant genus commonly known as burdock, is native to Europe and Asia. Plants of this genus grow prickly seedpods called burrs. The little hooks on the burrs easily cling to the fabrics of human clothing and the fur of wildlife. By hitchhiking on clothing and animals, the burrs move to new locations where they can spread their seeds.

HOOK AND LOOP FASTENER

In 1941, George de Mestral, a Swiss engineer, and his dog returned from a walk in the woods. Both his pants and his dog's coat were covered in burrs. Curious, de Mestral examined the burrs under a microscope and observed their hook-like shape. This led to his idea for a two-sided fastener, one side with tiny hooks and the other with loops to catch them. De Mestral named his hook and loop fastener VELCRO®, from the French words *velours* (velvet) and *crochet* (hook).

ARMADILLO

Armadillos originated in South America, but today some live in Central America and the southern central states of North America. *Armadillo* means "little armored one" in Spanish. The "armor" of an armadillo is made of thick plates with overlapping scales composed of bone with a covering of horn. When threatened by predators, one species of armadillo hides by curling its head and feet back into its shell and rolling up into a hard ball.

FOLD-UP CAR

The Armadillo-T Car was developed in 2013 by a research team headed by In-Soo Suh at the Korea Advanced Institute of Science and Technology (KAIST). Their goal was to develop a space-efficient electric vehicle. The Armadillo-T Car mimics an armadillo by rolling into a ball-like shape. The rear of the car folds over the front, decreasing the length from 110 inches (2.8 meters) to 65 inches (1.7 meters). Drivers can park this car in high-density areas because it occupies much less space than a standard car.

SPONGES and CORALS

Sponges and corals are two kinds of animals that live in water. Sponges are found mostly in oceans, but some exist in freshwater. Corals live in large colonies in warm subtropical and tropical waters. Both sponges and corals are filter feeders. They eat microscopic prey by straining the surrounding water with mesh- or net-like body parts. They also improve water quality and clarity by filtering out particles and bacteria from the water.

SMOG-EATING SHELL

Mexico City has a high level of air pollution. In 2012, a decorative smog-eating facade, or shell, was installed on a building at the city's Manuel Gea González Hospital to help improve the air quality. Designed by the German architectural firm Elegant Embellishments, the facade tiles have a complex, irregular grid pattern based on sponges and corals. When activated by sunlight, a coating on the tiles acts as a filtration system to break down and neutralize smog and air pollutants.

OCTOPUS

Octopuses are believed to be intelligent invertebrates (animals without backbones). They have eight long, tapered, flexible arms that are powerful tools. Their arms can grip, twist, and change length and stiffness. Octopuses also have hundreds of suction cups on their arms that can form strong seals on all kinds of surfaces. Boneless, an octopus can adapt its body shape to its environment, squeeze into and out of tight spaces, and retrieve objects in narrow openings.

ROBOTIC ARM

The TentacleGripper is an octopus-inspired soft robotic arm. It was developed between 2015 and 2017 by Festo, a German company, in collaboration with the School of Mechanical Engineering and Automation at Beihang University in China. Made from flexible silicone, the tapered arm with suction cups can grip, lift, move, and set down irregularly shaped objects. This secure gripping method and the arm's soft, silicone material improve the safety of robotic systems in industrial workplaces and for homes.

STALACTITES and STALAGMITES

Stalactites and stalagmites are mineral formations found in caves. Stalactites hang down from above. They are formed over time when water drips through cracks in the cave ceiling. The water evaporates, and the minerals left behind build up on the ceiling to resemble icicles. Stalagmites grow upward when water that drips onto the floor of a cave evaporates and leaves mounds of minerals behind. Because the caves are dark and wet, they are naturally cool.

URBAN SPACE

An urban space called the Water Cathedral was a temporary installation in Santiago, Chile. GUN Architects, a Chilean-German firm, designed a cool, cave-like environment. Cone-shaped cloth stalactites above dripped water, and concrete stalagmites on the ground provided seating and water collection. The cathedral was the winner of a 2011 initiative by the Chile-based cultural platform CONSTRUCTO and New York's Museum of Modern Art (MoMA) to design a space that offered relief from the summer heat.

HONEYCOMB

Honeycomb is constructed by honeybees. Each bee makes a wax cylinder. When the cylinders are assembled in a hive, surface tension and the pressure of surrounding cylinders shape them into hexagons. The six-sided cells fit together tightly, with the walls supporting one another to make a space-efficient and sturdy structure. Although the hexagon shape uses the least amount of wax, a bee consumes 8 ounces (227 grams) of honey to produce 1 ounce (28 grams) of wax.

HOUSING PROJECT

In 2006, OFIS Architects won a competition for designing low-income housing for young families and couples in Slovenia. The prize-winning Honeycomb Apartments are constructed from modules that mimic the structure of honeycomb. The modules fit together tightly, creating apartments in a variety of sizes that are space and energy efficient. The colorful balconies provide privacy and shade, and perforated side panels allow for natural ventilation.

CAT EYES

Cats and some other animals that go out at night have eyes designed for low-light vision. These animals have a reflective surface behind the retina of each eye that helps them see in the dark. The surface functions like a mirror and bounces back whatever light is available, providing a second chance for the animal to see objects and movement. Some of the light also bounces back out of the animal's eyes. This reflected light is what causes the glowing appearance of the eyes.

ROAD REFLECTOR

One foggy night in 1933, Percy Shaw was driving home in Yorkshire, England. The poor visibility made Shaw struggle to keep his car on the road. Then two bright spots of light appeared. A cat's eyes shining in the headlights of his car helped Shaw avoid swerving off a steep edge. This experience sparked an idea. If he could invent a reflective device for road surfaces, it could guide drivers and improve road safety. The next year Shaw patented his own "cat's eye," a reflective road stud that is embedded in roadway pavement.

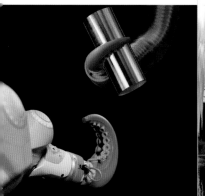

NATURE-INSPIRED DESIGN AND BIOMIMICRY

The pairings of illustrations and photographs in this book all show examples of nature-inspired design. Nature-inspired design occurs when people solve problems based on what they observe happening in nature, or when plant or animal behaviors or characteristics inspire new human inventions. Most of the pairings are also examples of biomimicry. The word biomimicry comes from two Greek words: *bios*, which means "life," and *mimesis*, which means "imitate." The Biomimicry Institute describes biomimicry as "a practice that learns from and mimics the strategies found in nature to solve human design challenges."

There are several myths and legends that reflect early examples of biomimicry. In one Greek myth, Daedalus, an inventor and a craftsperson, created wings, like those of a bird, from feathers bound together with wax. He strapped the wings to himself and his son, Icarus, so they could fly away and escape the island of Crete. Unfortunately, Icarus flew too close to the sun. The sun's heat melted the wax, destroying the wings, and Icarus fell into the sea.

Leonardo da Vinci (1452–1519), painter, scientist, inventor, and more, studied the flight of birds and bats. He sketched their body structures and then drew plans for flying machines that would enable humans to fly. He said, "Go take your lessons in nature, that's where our future is." Although none of da Vinci's machines succeeded, his ideas inspired the Wright brothers, who did create a successful flying machine.

Nature is a constant innovator, adapting and refining designs and processes to survive and thrive on our planet for 3.8 billion years. Any failures eventually changed or no longer exist. People today can learn from the natural world and become "copycats." Plant, animal, and natural patterns, designs, behaviors, and characteristics can provide inspiration to innovate. The goal is to create sustainable new products, processes, systems, and technologies that solve our greatest design challenges and create new ways of living in harmony with all life on Earth.

> "Biomimicry is . . .
> the conscious emulation of life's genius."
>
> —Janine Benyus, cofounder, Biomimicry Institute

Readers interested in biomimicry design may wish to join the Youth Design Challenge (YDC). Information can be found here: https://youthchallenge.biomimicry.org.

TANKA

The poems throughout this book are written in a form called tanka. Japanese poets developed this form over hundreds of years. The word *tanka* means "short song" or "short poem." Tanka developed from waka, poetry written by members of the Japanese court in the sixth century. By the late-eighth century, tanka became a synonym for waka. The poems originally were chanted aloud, and the subject matter ranged from nature to love. Today, tanka are written about any subject. Each tanka is a self-contained story.

Tanka is a poetry form with rules. In Japanese, tanka have thirty-one speech sounds, or syllables. Also in Japanese, a tanka is often written in one continuous line without any punctuation. In English, the tanka form is different. Tanka still have thirty-one syllables, but these syllables are written in five-line poems. Each of the five lines has a required number of syllables. The first line has five syllables, the second line has seven syllables, the third line has five syllables, and the last two lines have seven syllables each. The structure of lines and the syllable counts are as follows:

Line 1: five syllables

Line 2: seven syllables

Line 3: five syllables

Line 4: seven syllables

Line 5: seven syllables

Tanka usually do not have titles and do not rhyme. There is no capitalization at the beginning and no period at the end. Throughout there is very little or no punctuation.

In this book's tanka, the third line of each poem has a special purpose. It serves as a turning point or bridge and is called a pivot. The content of the pivot relates to both the first two lines and the last two lines. The pivot line thereby joins or links the first two lines to the last two lines to tell a complete story.

Since the theme of this book is nature-inspired design, the tanka focus on nature and design. The first two lines of each poem describe a behavior or strategy in nature, and the last two lines highlight the human response of innovative design or invention. The third line, the pivot, links them.

SOURCES*

Lotus Leaf / Umbrella

Brightman, Sarah. "Reflections Under the Lotus Leaf." *Nature Meets Culture Stories* (blog). https://naturemeetsculturestories.wordpress.com/2016/06/14/lotus-leaf/.

"Interesting Umbrella Facts." Umbrella History. http://www.umbrellahistory.net/umbrella-facts/interesting-facts-about-umbrellas/.

"Origin of the Umbrella." China Umbrella Museum. https://www.hisour.com/origin-of-the-umbrella-china-umbrella-museum-48261/.

Schreiner, Wyatt. "Biomimicry: A History." OSU.EDU, Department of History ehistory. https://ehistory.osu.edu/exhibitions/biomimicry-a-history.

Symons, Esme, ed. "Superhydrophobicity, from Leaf to Lab." *Science Borealis* (blog), July 27, 2020. https://blog.scienceborealis.ca/superhydrophobicity-from-leaf-to-lab/.

Dragonfly / Helicopter

"Dragonflies Defy Evolution." Exploration Films, May 7, 2008. http://www.youtube.com/watch?v=4IOD5NEV-Kw.

"First Ideas About Vertical Flight." Heli Start. http://www.helistart.com/HeliHistoryFirstIdeas.aspx.

Kautt, Caleb and Johanna Kautt. "Helicopters and Dragonflies." *Copying the Creator* (blog), October 2011. https://cetministries.files.wordpress.com/2011/04/sep-oct-2011-copying-the-creator-helicopters-and-dragonflies.pdf.

Peltier, John. "Igor Sikorsky Built His First Helicopter Before the Wrights Flew." *Disciples of Flight* (blog). https://disciplesofflight.com/igor-sikorsky-first-helicopter/.

"This Day in Aviation History—First Tethered Flight of the Vought-Sikorsky VS-300." *Warbird Digest*, September 14, 2021. https://warbirdsnews.com/warbird-articles/this-day-in-aviation-history-first-tethered-flight-of-the-vought-sikorsky-vs-300.html.

Baobab / Vertical Garden

Shales, Melissa. "The Baobab: Fun Facts About Africa's Tree of Life." ThoughtCo., December 3, 2019. https://www.thoughtco.com/fun-facts-about-the-baobab-tree-1454374.

"Singapore's Gardens by the Bay." Archello. https://archello.com/project/gardens-by-the-bay#stories.

"Solar Trees in City Gardens (Singapore)." Solaripedia. https://www.solaripedia.com/13/416/solar_trees_in_city_gardens_(singapore).html.

"Supertrees, Gardens by the Bay." Grant Associates. https://grant-associates.uk.com/projects/supertrees-gardens-by-the-bay.

"The Baobab Tree: Africa's Iconic Tree of Life." *Aduna* (blog). https://aduna.com/blogs/learn/the-baobab-tree.

Velazquez, Linda. "Featured Project: Gardens by the Bay Supertrees." Greenroofs.com, October 20, 2020. https://www.greenroofs.com/2020/10/20/featured-project-gardens-by-the-bay-supertrees/.

Desert Beetle / Water Bottle

Clark, Liat. "This Self-filling Water Bottle Mimics a Desert Beetle." *Wired*, November 26, 2012. https://www.wired.com/2012/11/namib-beetle-bottle/.

"Namib Desert Beetle." Weebly. https://dewbankbeetle.weebly.com/namib-desert-beetle.html.

Seth, Radhika. "Beetle Juice Inspired!" YD: Yanko Design, July 5, 2010. https://www.yankodesign.com/2010/07/05/beetle-juice-inspired/.

Stewart, Lea. "Beetle-Inspired Bottle Harvests Drinking Water from Thin Air." *Inhabitat*, July 7, 2010. https://inhabitat.com/beetle-inspired-bottle-harvests-drinking-water-from-thin-air/.

Summers, Adam. "Like Water Off a Beetle's Back." *Natural History*, February 2004. https://www.naturalhistorymag.com/biomechanics/171934/like-water-off-a-beetle-s-back.

Kingfisher / Bullet Train

Bangor University. "Researching the Kingfisher's Hydrodynamic Design." *Journal of The Royal Society Interface*, May 15, 2019. https://phys.org/news/2019-05-kingfisher-hydrodynamic.html.

JR-West. "High Speed Train Inspired by the Kingfisher." Ask Nature, 1997. https://asknature.org/innovation/high-speed-train-inspired-by-the-kingfisher/.

Li, Jolie. "Shinkansen: The Bullet Train Inspired by Kingfishers." UX Collective. https://uxdesign.cc/shinkansen-the-bullet-train-inspired-by-kingfishers-bf6173cc5eae.

McKeag, Tom. "How One Engineer's Birdwatching Made Japan's Bullet Train Better." GreenBiz, October 19, 2012. https://www.greenbiz.com/article/how-one-engineers-birdwatching-made-japans-bullet-train-better.

Stier, Sam. "The Beak That Inspired a Bullet Train: Kingfishers." Ask Nature. https://asknature.org/strategy/beak-provides-streamlining/.

Snail / Desert Dwelling

Clendaniel, Morgan. "A Self-cooling Desert Dwelling, Inspired by the Lowly Snail." *Fast Company*, March 13, 2012. https://www.fastcompany.com/90181998/a-self-cooling-desert-dwelling-inspired-by-the-lowly-snail.

Laylin, Tafline. "Curvy Desert Home Designed by Iranian Students Mimics the Snail." Green Prophet, March 15, 2012. https://www.greenprophet.com/2012/03/iran-desert-mimics-snail/.

Liorhobashi. "Learning From the Desert Snail." *Spatial Experiments* (blog), September 20, 2016. https://spatialexperiments.wordpress.com/2016/09/20/learning-from-the-desert-snail/.

"Shell Protects from Heat." Ask Nature, September 13, 2016. https://asknature.org/strategy/shell-protects-from-heat/.

Hummingbird / Wind Converter

Arif, Aayesha. "This Small-Scale Wind Turbine Inspired by Hummingbird Wings Can Generate 1 KW of Power." *Wonderful Engineering* (blog), August 13, 2017. https://wonderfulengineering.com/wind-turbine-hummingbird-wings/.

Laylin, Tafline. "Revolutionary Flapping Wind Turbine Mimics Hummingbirds to Produce Clean Energy." *Inhabitat*, January 29, 2017. https://inhabitat.com/revolutionary-flapping-wind-turbine-mimics-hummingbirds-to-produce-clean-energy/.

Mayntz, Melissa. "Guide to Hummingbird Flight." The Spruce, March 13, 2021. https://www.thespruce.com/how-hummingbirds-fly-386446.

Yong, Ed. "Hummingbird Flight Has a Clever Twist." *Nature*, December 14, 2011. https://www.nature.com/articles/nature.2011.9639.

Termite Mound / Building Complex

Dillon, Matt and Phil Wilkinson. "Mr Resilience." Ecolibrium Feature, October 2009. https://www.airah.org.au/Content_Files/EcoLibrium/2009/October09/2009-10-F03.pdf.

Fehrenbacher, Jill. "Biomimetic Architecture: Green Building in Zimbabwe Modeled After Termite Mounds." *Inhabitat*, November 29, 2012. https://inhabitat.com/building-modelled-on-termites-eastgate-centre-in-zimbabwe/.

Pearce, Mick. "Of Termites and Architecture." https://www.mickpearce.com/biomimicry.html.

Turner, J. Scott and Rupert C. Soar. "Beyond Biomimicry: What Termites Can Tell Us About Realizing the Living Building." First International Conference on Industrialized, Intelligent Construction (I3CON), Loughborough University, May 14–16, 2008. https://www.esf.edu/efb/turner/publication%20pdfs/Beyond%20Biomimicry%20MS%20distribution.pdf.

Wolverton, Mark. "What Termites Can Teach Engineers." ASME: The American Society of Mechanical Engineers, November 21, 2019. https://www.asme.org/topics-resources/content/what-termites-can-teach-engineers.

Burrs / Hook and Loop Fastener

Daniels, Patricia. "The Invention of Velcro." ThoughtCo., January 23, 2020. https://www.thoughtco.com/the-invention-of-velcro-4066111.

Schreiner, Wyatt. "Biomimicry: A History." OSU.EDU, Department of History ehistory. https://ehistory.osu.edu/exhibitions/biomimicry-a-history.

Stephens, Thomas. "How a Swiss Invention Hooked the World." SWI: Swissinfo.ch, January 4, 2007. https://www.swissinfo.ch/eng/velcro_how-a-swiss-invention-hooked-the-world/5653568.

Swearingen, Jake. "An Idea That Stuck: How George de Mestral Invented the Velcro Fastener." The Vindicated. https://nymag.com/vindicated/2016/11/an-idea-that-stuck-how-george-de-mestral-invented-velcro.html.

*All web content and hyperlinks were live at the time of original publication. The author and publisher do not assume responsibility for any changes made since that time.

Armadillo / Fold-Up Car

Andrews, Kate. "Armadillo-T Foldable Electric Micro-car by KAIST." *Dezeen*, August 23, 2013. https://www.dezeen.com/2013/08/23/armadillo-t-foldable-electric-micro-car-by-kaist/.

"Armadillos." A B C All Wildlife Removal. http://abcallwildlife.com/wildlife%20pest%20control%20armadillos.htm.

"Armadillos." Havahart. https://www.havahart.com/armadillo-facts.

Choudhury, Nilima. "South Korea Launches 'Armadillo' Folding Electric Car." Climate Home News, August 22, 2013. https://www.climatechangenews.com/2013/08/22/south-korea-launches-armadillo-folding-electric-car/.

"La Plata Three-banded Armadillo." Smithsonian's National Zoo & Conservation Biology Institute. https://nationalzoo.si.edu/animals/la-plata-three-banded-armadillo.

Treuhaft, Teshia. "Shrinking Cars for an Expanding Population: KAIST's Armadillo-T." Core77, August 29, 2013. https://www.core77.com/posts/25433/Shrinking-Cars-for-an-Expanding-Populations-KAISTs-Armadillo-T#.

Sponges and Corals / Smog-Eating Shell

Admin. "Depolluting Quasicrystal Facade Cleans Mexico City's Air." *eVolo*, April 5, 2013. http://www.evolo.us/depolluting-quasicrystal-facade-cleans-mexico-citys-air/.

Burke, Travis and Marios Alexandrou, ed. "Filter Feeders and Anemones." Infolific: Pets & Animals. https://infolific.com/pets/coral-reef-life/filter-feeders-and-anemones/.

"Corals v Sponges (What are Corals)." Animal Creative Facts, April 23, 2021. https://animalcreativefacts.com/corals-vs-sponges/.

Green, Jetson. "Decorative Facade Removes Air Pollution in Perth, Mexico City, and Abu Dhabi." Avada, May 15, 2013. https://www.jetsongreen.com/2013/05/decorative-facade-removes-air-pollution-in-perth-mexico-city-and-abu-dhabi.html.

Kokturk, Gulden and Tutku Didem Akyol Altun, eds. "Smog-eating Facades." *Interdisciplinary Expansions in Engineering and Design with the Power of Biomimicry*, March 2018. https://books.google.com/books?id=R-mPDwAAQBAJ&pg=PA928&lpg=PA928&dq="Smog-eating+Facades."+Interdisciplinary+Expansions+in+Engineering+and+Design+with+the+Power+of+Biomimicry&source=bl&ots=eRzeDg8Cqu&sig=ACfU3UlyOLFpoRvnta-LihNjIThDxsOnoA&hl=en&sa=X&ved=2ahUKEwiewl_Py4TIAhXzGDQIHZhLCPwQ6AF6BAgdEAM#v=onepage&q="Smog-eating%20Facades."%20Interdisciplinary%20Expansions%20in%20Engineering%20and%20Design%20with%20the%20Power%20of%20Biomimicry&f=false.

Nakaya, Rion. "Ocean Sponges Have Incredible Filtering Power." TKSST: The Kids Should See This. https://thekidshouldseethis.com/post/ocean-sponges-have-incredible-filtering-power-a-demo-with-dye.

Octopus / Robotic Arm

Burrows, Leah. "The Tentacle Bot: Octopus-inspired Robot Can Grip, Move, and Manipulate a Wide Range of Objects." Harvard School of Engineering and Applied Sciences, February 27, 2020. https://www.seas.harvard.edu/news/2020/02/tentacle-bot.

"Octopus Facts." Facts Just for Kids. https://www.factsjustforkids.com/animal-facts/octopus-facts-for-kids/.

Owano, Nancy. "Octopus Tentacle Serves as Inspiration for Gripper." Tech Xplore, March 31, 2017. https://techxplore.com/news/2017-03-octopus-tentacle-gripper.html.

"Tentacle Gripper: Gripping Modelled on an Octopus Tentacle." FESTO. https://www.festo.com/net/SupportPortal/Files/630182/Festo_TentacleGripper_en.pdf.

Xie, Zhexin and August G. Domel, Ning An, Connor Green, Zheyuan Gong, Tianmiao Wang, Elias M. Knubben, James C. Weaver, Katia Bertoldi, and Li Wen. "Octopus Arm-Inspired Tapered Soft Actuators with Suckers for Improved Grasping." *Soft Robotics* 7, no. 5 (October 16, 2020): 639–648, https://www.liebertpub.com/doi/10.1089/soro.2019.0082.

Stalactites and Stalagmites / Urban Space

Architectural Review Editors. "Chilean Water Cathedral by GUN Architects, Santiago." *The Architectural Review*, November 23, 2012. https://www.architectural-review.com/today/chilean-water-cathedral-by-gun-architects-santiago.

Carpentieri, Romina. "Water Cathedral/Gun Architects." Formakers™. http://www.formakers.eu/project-429-gun-architects-water-cathedral.

"Gun Architects: Water Cathedral." Designboom. https://www.designboom.com/architecture/gun-architects-water-cathedral/.

Sieverson, Diane. "Stalactities & Stalagmites Lesson for Kids." Study.com. https://study.com/academy/lesson/stalactites-stalagmites-lesson-for-kids.html.

"Speleology. Stalactites and Stalagmites." CaveHaven. https://cavehaven.com/stalactites-and-stalagmites/.

Honeycomb / Housing Project

Carstens, Andy. "Honeycomb Structure Is Space-Efficient and Strong: Bees and Wasps." https://asknature.org/strategy/honeycomb-structure-is-space-efficient-and-strong/.

Dalil, Mehdi. "Why Do Bees Love Hexagons?" UX Collective, June 1, 2020. https://uxdesign.cc/why-do-bees-love-hexagons-119cfd0d95a9.

"Izola Social Housing/OFIS arhitekti." *ArchDaily*, June 30, 2008. https://www.archdaily.com/3245/izola-social-housing-ofis-arhitekti.

Krulwich, Robert. "What Is It About Bees and Hexagons?" NPR, May 14, 2013. https://www.npr.org/sections/krulwich/2013/05/13/183704091/what-is-it-about-bees-and-hexagons.

Yoneda, Yuka. "Housing Complex in Slovenia Is a Series of Honeycomb Modular Apartments." *Inhabitat*, February 1, 2011. https://inhabitat.com/slovenias-gorgeous-honeycomb-housing-complex/.

Cat Eyes / Road Reflector

Irish, Vivien. "Percy Shaw." *YPS: Yorkshire Philosophical Society* (blog). https://www.ypsyork.org/resources/yorkshire-scientists-and-innovators/percy-shaw/.

"Meowfest: Why Do Cat Eyes Glow in the Dark?" Carnegie Museum of Natural History. https://carnegiemnh.org/meowfest-why-do-cat-eyes-glow-in-the-dark/.

Plester, Jeremy. "Weatherwatch: Percy Shaw and the Invention of the Cat's Eye Reflector." *The Guardian*, December 3, 2018. https://www.theguardian.com/news/2018/dec/03/weatherwatch-percy-shaw-and-the-invention-of-the-cats-eye-reflector.

Seabrook, Andrea. "Why Do Animals' Eyes Glow in the Dark?" NPR, October 31, 2008. https://www.npr.org/templates/story/story.php?storyId=96414364.

Nature-Inspired Design and Biomimicry

Benyus, Janine M. *Biomimicry: Innovation Inspired by Nature*. New York: William Morrow, 1997.

Biomimicry Collection. Ask Nature. https://asknature.org/?s=What%20is%20Biomimicry%3F&page=0&is_v=1.

Biomimicry Institute. https://biomimicry.org/what-is-biomimicry/.

Gregory, Josh. *From Woodpeckers to … Helmets* (21st Century Skills Innovation Library: Innovations from Nature). Ann Arbor, MI: Cherry Lake Publishing, 2013.

Harman, Jay. *The Shark's Paintbrush: Biomimicry and How Nature Is Inspiring Innovation*. Ashland, OR: White Cloud Press, 2013.

Lee, Dora. *Biomimicry: Inventions Inspired by Nature*. Toronto: Kids Can Press, 2011.

Mara, Wil. *From Cats' Eyes to … Reflectors* (21st Century Skills Innovation Library: Innovations from Nature). Ann Arbor, MI: Cherry Lake Publishing, 2013.

———. *From Kingfishers to … Bullet Trains* (21st Century Skills Innovation Library: Innovations from Nature). Ann Arbor, MI: Cherry Lake Publishing, 2013.

Schreiner, Wyatt. "Biomimicry: A History." OSU.EDU, Department of History ehistory. https://ehistory.osu.edu/exhibitions/biomimicry-a-history.

Thompson, Richard. *Nature's Design: Exploring the Mysteries of the Natural World*. Cape Town: Struik Nature/Random House, 2008.

Tanka

Emrich, Jeanne. "A Quick Start Guide to Writing Tanka." Tanka Online. https://www.tankaonline.com/Quick%20Start%20Guide.htm.

Fielden, Amelia. "About Tanka and Its History." Tanka Online. https://www.tankaonline.com/About%20Tanka%20and%20Its%20History.htm.

"Tanka." Britannica Kids. https://kids.britannica.com/students/article/tanka/629308.

"Tanka." Poets.org. https://poets.org/glossary/tanka.

"Tanka and the Five W's." *Graceguts* (blog). https://sites.google.com/site/graceguts/essays/tanka-and-the-five-ws.

ACKNOWLEDGMENTS

Thanks to teacher extraordinaire and friend Carolyn Rubenstein, who introduced me to the notion of biomimicry, and to Jill Eisenberg, who encouraged me to develop a book about nature-inspired design. Grateful appreciation to Rosanna Ayers, Director of Youth Education, Biomimicry Institute, as well as to AskNature and Innovation at the Biomimicry Institute (TBI); and to Ann Spiers, member of Haiku Northwest, for reviewing the backmatter in this book. Thanks to John Willson, Vera Michalchik, Christine Brunner, and my husband, Scott Apostolou, for helping me connect with resources and consultants. Thanks also to my writers group: Debbie Duncan, Kirk Glaser, Cynthia Chin-Lee, Mark Reibstein, and Kevin and SuAnn Kiser; to my illustrators group: Lisa Brown, Katherine Tillotson, Susan Gal, Ashley Wolff, and especially Julie Downing, who photographed supertrees in Singapore for me; to my designer/art director daughter, Kate Apostolou, who has a keen eye; and to my editor, Louise May, on whom I rely to help give form to my ideas. And finally, thanks to the generous inventors and designers who shared photographs of their work for this book.

PHOTOGRAPH CREDITS

Road Reflector: Andrew Fox/Alamy Stock Photo; Child walking in rain (Umbrella): Rasstock/Shutterstock; Sikorsky VS-300 helicopter: © The Royal Aeronautical Society (National Aerospace Collection: Mary Evans Picture Library Ltd); Supertrees (Vertical Garden): Courtesy of Julie Downing; Dew Bank (Water) Bottle: Courtesy of Kitae Pak; Shinkansen (Bullet Train): Picture Partners/Alamy Stock Photo; Desert Dwelling: Courtesy of Rosa Atarod; Wind Converter: Courtesy of Anis Anouini/Tyer Wind; Eastgate Centre (Building Complex): Courtesy of David Brazier Photographer; Hook and Loop Fastener (VELCRO®): Stocksnapper; Armadillo-T (Fold-Up) Car: Courtesy of In-Soo Suh and the Korean Advanced Institute of Science and Technology (KAIST); Smog-Eating Shell: Courtesy of Elegant Embellishments LTD.; TentacleGripper (Robotic Arm): Courtesy of Festo; Water Cathedral (Urban Space): YAP_CONSTRUCTO 2: Water Cathedral by Gun Architects. Photograph: Guy Wenborne/Copyright: Constructo; Honeycomb Apartments (Housing Project): Courtesy of Tomaz Gregorič for OFIS Architects.

VELCRO® is a registered trademark of Velcro IP Holdings LLC. Used with permission.

For Jill and Louise

Edited by Louise E. May
Designed by Christy Hale
Production by The Kids at Our House
The text is set in Obviously Regular and Obviously Narrow
The illustrations are rendered as relief prints with digital layering

Manufactured in China by RR Donnelley
10 9 8 7 6 5 4 3 2 1
First Edition

Library of Congress Cataloging-in-Publication Data
Names: Hale, Christy, author, illustrator.
Title: Copycat : nature-inspired design around the world / Christy Hale.
Description: First edition. | New York : Lee & Low Books Inc., [2022] | Includes bibliographical references. | Audience: Ages 7-11 |
Summary: "A collection of tanka poems, illustrations, and photographs explore biomimicry and show how plants, animals, and objects in the natural world have inspired human-made inventions. Includes additional backmatter information about biomimicry, tanka, and the natural and human-made objects featured"— Provided by publisher.
Identifiers: LCCN 2021047193 | ISBN 9781643792309 (hardcover) ISBN 9781643794747 (ebk)
Subjects: LCSH: Biomimicry—Juvenile works. | Nature photography—Juvenile works. | Waka, American—Juvenile literature.
Classification: LCC TA164 .H34 2022 | DDC 660.6—dc23/eng/20211005
LC record available at https://lccn.loc.gov/2021047193